ONE

MIND · HEART · PURPOSE · GOAL

**The Official Commemorative of the
Super Bowl Champion Green Bay Packers**

FOREWORD BY CHARLES WOODSON   **INTRODUCTION BY** MIKE McCARTHY   **AFTERWORD BY** MARK MURPHY

PHOTOGRAPHY BY JAMES V. BIEVER, MICHAEL BIEVER, PEPPER BURRUSS, CHRIS CALLIES,
JEFFERY PHELPS, AARON POPKEY, JAMES D. SMITH, AND HARMANN STUDIOS

TABLE OF CONTENTS

FOREWORD Charles Woodson

We've got to think about one thing: *One.*

For two weeks, think about one. Let's be one mind, let's be one heartbeat, with one purpose, one goal, for one more game. *One. Let's get it.*

Now check this: The president doesn't want to come watch us at the Super Bowl? Guess what? We'll go see him!

Let's hear it: White House on three. *One, two, three—White House!*

I've never been a very vocal, outspoken guy. It's always been my thing to lead by example and let the guys see how I play. It just so happened that this year, during the playoffs, when it came time to decide who was going to talk to the team the guys said, "Hey, Charles will do it," and the duty fell to me.

I'm not scared to talk in front of people nor am I shy about it. It's just that I like to pick and choose when—and if—I say something. And if I do, I want it to mean something.

Looking back, it was an honor and a responsibility I took to heart. During a playoff run like we had, words should grow more meaningful with each successive victory, but I never expected the speech I gave in the Soldier Field locker room to carry the significance that it has. You can't predict something like that. But once Sam Shields intercepted that ball and we had the NFC Championship locked up, I started thinking about what to say that might stick with the guys for the next couple weeks until we got to the Super Bowl.

Having been to the Super Bowl before with the Oakland Raiders eight years prior, I knew all of the different distractions that come with it. I also knew that in my 13th year in the league, having never won one, there were no guarantees there would ever be another opportunity—for me or for the youngest guy on the team. So I wanted to put in the guys' minds that the next two weeks needed to be about this team, about this chance, and that's all we should be focused on.

As it turned out, the next time I talked to the team was more emotional. We were winning the Super Bowl at halftime, but I had fractured my collarbone and couldn't finish the game.

I broke down and could barely get any words out. If the guys had been inspired at all by the One speech, then at that moment they definitely saw how passionate I was about being in the Super Bowl. I think they understood how much it really meant to me. Hopefully, at that moment, it meant as much to them as well—to go out and seal this deal, because if you win it you're a champion forever.

It's special that the One speech has lived on in different ways. President Obama referenced it when we visited the White House—but I think he had to address it. I kind of made it personal for him, and our team went out there and made my words a statement of fact. But I think that made our visit different from everybody else's visit, and to go back and forth on stage making jokes with the president made it a pretty cool day for us.

Until I saw the Super Bowl rings, I had no clue that those words—Heart, Mind, Purpose, Goal—along with the number 1 would be etched inside. It's overwhelming. It means that you did your part to achieve something great. It lets you know that you somehow had an impact on the journey. It's something that will live forever.

Mike McCarthy

I t was 10:30 a.m., Super Bowl Sunday. I was standing outside the Mandalay East Ballroom at the Omni Mandalay Hotel, our team's headquarters for Super Bowl week, about to give the speech every coach has prepared for since the beginning of his career. It was now time to give my message for Super Bowl XLV.

When I walked in and looked at the players and coaches, they were bright-eyed and focused. I knew we would walk out that door with full confidence. I began by reminding the team how we reached this point and spoke of what was ahead.

I felt we won the preparation prize throughout the two weeks. I commended the players for their extensive film study and quality practices. It gave me great confidence in every individual in the room prior to the biggest game of the year. I truly believed we were ready to be successful against the Pittsburgh Steelers.

A few reminders were stated, then I went into the true message: *one*. I read the dictionary definition of the word *one*: being a single unit; being one in particular; being the same in kind or quality; a unified entity of two or more components; being in agreement or union.

One truly exemplified what our team had become.

There are three letters in the word one, just like the three components of our team. To win the Super Bowl, it would take all three phases—offense, defense, and special teams—working as one.

Then I related the word one to our team identity, which is emphasized every week during the season. Our identity was based on three components, all working as one: discipline, toughness, and sound fundamentals. It was important for our team to exhibit each of those characteristics.

Throughout the game plan, we felt discipline was the No. 1 priority in our team identity. A disciplined performance would be a major key to our victory. Our opponent was a strong, physical football team, but "Packer toughness" is evident in all areas of our play. Lastly, I spoke of being fundamentally sound, the basic foundation of successful football. That is our identity. We were prepared, and it was time to go play our game.

A baseball analogy fit the moment, and we watched a highlight from the film *The Natural*. It illustrated what our team was getting ready to face. It was the bottom of the ninth inning, and they were getting ready to send their big, right-handed pitcher to the mound. Ironically, "Pittsburgh" was written across the chest of his jersey. There had been blood spilled along the way. I told them, "We're in the batter's box, batting left-handed." I said we'd take the favorable side of the plate, jokingly, because we were favored in the game. We knew the pitch would be a fastball, because that's the way the Steelers play. It was time to trust our preparation. It was time to trust our process. It was time to hit the homerun into the right field lights.

I told the team we were playing for the World Championship because we belonged there. The key to our successful journey was our players: no one needed to change, no one needed to be different. We were in North Texas because we earned it, every step of the way. It was a hard and different way at times, but there we were, and we weren't going to change. We were fully comfortable with who we were.

We carried the history and tradition of the Green Bay Packers on Super Bowl Sunday, but more importantly the brand of the 2010 Packers.

"Wear the green jerseys proudly," was the message to the 45 warriors who would play. The responsibility fell on the rest of us to support them. It was time to claim what was ours.

I concluded by reminding them what Charles Woodson said best after the NFC Championship win in Chicago. We are *One* Mind, *One* Heart, *One* Purpose, *One* Goal. I wanted to make clear why we were there, to claim the trophy that belongs in one city: Green Bay. It had one name on it: Lombardi. Super Bowl XLV was our time. It was time to take the Lombardi Trophy home.

The photos and stories that follow will always serve as a reminder of how special the 2010 season was. They are a tribute to the players on that team, and show moments of triumph and moments that we would have to overcome. They are stories that needed to be told and plays that shouldn't be forgotten. I will always admire our consistency, through all the challenges, and the way we stood up to each one of them.

The following pages relive the moments of a special season when a team and its fans became *One*. Enjoy.

27

	1	2	3	4
PACKERS	0	13	14	0
EAGLES	3	0	7	10

20

After dominating the Eagles with three sacks, knocking their starting quarterback from the game, and leading the charge in stopping a critical fourth-and-1 late in the fourth quarter, linebacker Clay Matthews was just being honest in assessing his season-opening performance.

"I didn't think I played my best ball," he said.

A confessed smart aleck, Matthews wasn't being snide in this case. He had missed the entire preseason with a troublesome hamstring injury and hadn't played a game in eight months. Having chased first Kevin Kolb and then Michael Vick all over Lincoln Financial Field, Matthews needed a breather in the fourth quarter following a sack of Vick, and he was shown on the sidelines nearly buckled over from exhaustion.

But after one play and the two-minute warning, Matthews returned to the defensive huddle for the big fourth-and-1 at the Green Bay 42-yard line and outfoxed two blockers at the point of attack to snuff out Vick's shotgun keeper. The stop preserved the Packers' 27-20 victory and launched Matthews' sophomore season in impressive fashion.

Matthews went on to notch three more sacks the following week, earn his second straight Pro Bowl bid and pick up a host of awards along the way.

"He is a beast," cornerback Charles Woodson said. "He is one of those guys that is never going to give up on a play, and it is hard to block him if you try to block him with one guy.

"We see it every day. He is a monster. He gives people fits."

The city of Philadelphia had done the same to the Packers for nearly a half-century, and the loss of running back Ryan Grant to a season-ending ankle injury made this an especially costly victory. But the triumph was Green Bay's first in Philly since 1962, and it made returning to the City of Brotherly Love four months later for a playoff showdown far less daunting than it otherwise might have been.

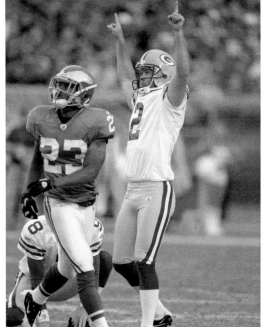

> " Finally. We've had a lot of heartbreaks on this field. Fourth-and-26, a lot of other different situations. It feels good to leave this field, finally, with a win. "
> – LB Nick Barnett

		1	2	3	4	
BILLS	7	0	7	0	0	
PACKERS		13	0	14	7	34

Jermichael Finley has always heard he's a wide receiver in a tight end's body, and the Packers' rising star reminded everyone in Week 2 just how dangerous that combination can be.

The Buffalo Bills couldn't cover Finley. It didn't matter whether they used a linebacker, a safety, or a cornerback, and it didn't matter the route, whether Finley was cutting across the middle or taking off up the seam.

Finley caught just four passes in the Packers' 34-7 blowout win, but it was the damage he did with them that mattered, as he racked up 103 yards receiving for an average of better than 25 yards per grab.

He even missed a chance to make what would have been one of the biggest plays of his career, when he was wide open deep downfield off a play-action fake for a potential 57-yard touchdown had quarterback Aaron Rodgers not thrown to Jordy Nelson for 15 yards instead.

"I don't think I've been ... in my life that open," Finley said. "I think I probably could have done karaoke and got in the end zone still. But we got the first down and that's all that counts."

The next week, Finley burned the Chicago defense for nine catches and 115 yards, his third 100-yard performance in a span of four games dating back to the 2009 NFC Wild Card playoff at Arizona. He was off to the best start by a tight end in franchise annals with 301 yards through four games in 2010, making it a travesty he was injured in Week 5 and unable to resume a potentially historic individual season.

Finley was thrilled the Packers went on to win the Super Bowl but obviously bummed to only be an interested observer. He's sure to play a bigger role in whatever 2011 brings.

> " We're trying to achieve greatness out there. We're not trying to be average, we're not trying to be the second runner. We're trying to be No. 1. "
>
> – TE Jermichael Finley

23

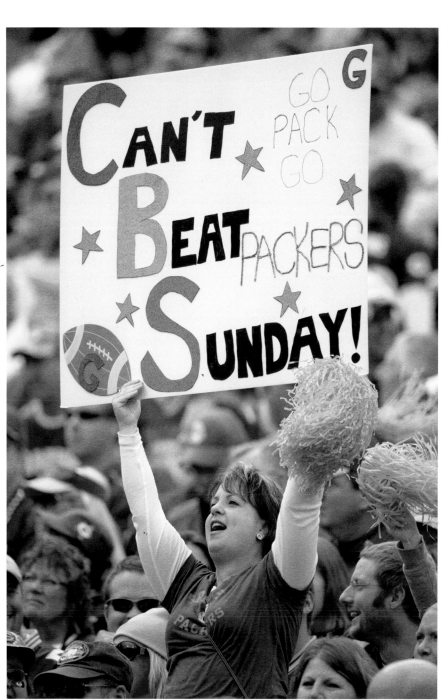

 **17**

	1	2	3	4
PACKERS	7	3	0	7
BEARS	0	7	0	13

20

For the dejected Packers in the visiting locker room at Soldier Field, it felt like more than just a game that got away. It felt like a potential victory that was given away haphazardly, with green gift wrap and a big yellow bow. After a performance full of miscues and blunders and committing a team-record 18 penalties, the Packers were left pondering what could have been.

Green Bay had been flagged a combined eight times in the first two contests, but was undermined by 152 penalty yards in Chicago. There were other culprits that contributed to the defeat—special teams breakdowns and untimely turnovers—despite the Packers outgaining the Bears by over 100 yards and possessing the ball more than 11 minutes longer than Chicago.

It was the kind of night where the Packers would make a heroic goal-line stand at their own 1 in the second half and immediately commit three pre-snap penalties with the offensive linemen's feet in the end zone. On the ensuing punt, the Bears' Devin Hester would weave through Green Bay's coverage for a 62-yard touchdown. Earlier in the third quarter, Chicago blocked a field goal attempt after a touchdown was wiped out moments before by a holding infraction.

Following Hester's return, the Packers retook the lead in the fourth quarter, 17-14. On the Bears' next possession, the defense appeared to come up with a huge turnover, but it was nullified by a penalty, keeping alive a Chicago march that led to a game-tying field goal. Green Bay's promising final drive concluded with a fumble by wide receiver James Jones at midfield.

On Chicago's final possession, Nick Collins intercepted Jay Cutler, but was another positive negated by a penalty. The Bears concluded the short march with a 19-yard chip shot by kicker Rob Gould with four seconds left.

The penalties had Head Coach Mike McCarthy fuming. It was also a lesson learned. The Packers averaged four penalties per contest for the remainder of 2010.

"It's disappointing to give away a game like this. We're not Santa Claus. We're not in the business of jumping down your chimney and letting you have a game."

– LB Nick Barnett

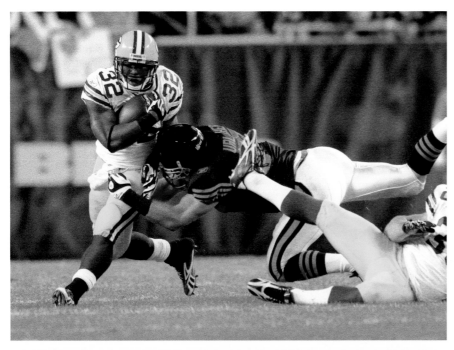

	1	2	3	4
LIONS	0	14	6	6
PACKERS	7	14	7	0

26   **28**

GAME 4

SUNDAY, OCTOBER 3, 2010
Lambeau Field • Attendance 70,729

It was a patient strut back to the bench, ball in one palm, teammates celebrating wildly around him, after Charles Woodson scored his team-record ninth defensive TD on a 48-yard interception return that he punctuated by diving into the end zone. It exuded the ancient football adage "act like you've been there before," because of course the 13-year veteran had, more than all but a few defenders in NFL history.

Woodson's touchdown early in the third quarter pushed the Packers ahead, 28-14, and it seemed to put Detroit on its heels for good. But the scrappy Lions were improved from past years, and rallied to cut the lead to 28-26 in the fourth quarter. It paved the way for more Woodson heroics on Detroit's final drive, with the cornerback making three crucial plays.

He knifed through the line of scrimmage to drop running back Jahvid Best for a 1-yard gain at the Green Bay 37 on first down before breaking up consecutive passes to towering wide receiver Calvin Johnson on the next two plays, forcing a punt. The Packers were able to run out the remaining 6:32 with a 12-play drive to clinch the victory.

In a career filled with memorable moments, it was a milestone performance for Woodson. He became the only player in NFL history to return an interception for a touchdown for five straight seasons, and also the first in league record books to have an interception return for a TD against the same team three consecutive years.

The following week, while sitting in an empty locker room with a painted game ball wrapped in cellophane behind him commemorating his efforts vs. Detroit, Woodson summed up the game, his achievements and his career in one brief thought.

"You start thinking about your legacy when you get toward the end of your career," he said. "That's something I think about. It's why I play so hard. I want people to say, 'He left it all on the field.'"

> "With everything that had gone wrong up to that point, the last three plays on defense, Charles Woodson makes all three of them. And then we get the ball back and we control it for 12 plays and end the game. Those last 15 plays of the game I thought were impressive Packer football.
>
> – Head Coach Mike McCarthy

		1	2	3	4	OT	
	PACKERS	7	3	3	0	0	13
	REDSKINS	0	3	0	10	3	16

Mike McCarthy's post-game press conference began like a laundry list, delivered with an expressionless monotone that reflected neither despair nor indignation, but the even-keel demeanor that would serve the head coach well.

Matter of fact, the injuries had to be endured, both that day in a disappointing overtime defeat and for the rest of a season still viewed as promising.

Jermichael Finley, knee. Ryan Pickett, ankle. Donald Lee, shoulder. Clay Matthews, hamstring. Derrick Martin, knee. Aaron Rodgers, concussion. Finally McCarthy was done with the list, and the Packers would be forced to deal with the adversity.

"In all my years of playing, I've never seen anything like this," said Pickett, a 10-year veteran.

Finley and Martin wouldn't play again in 2010. Pickett missed two of the next three games. Nick Barnett, Mark Tauscher and Morgan Burnett had already missed this game due to injuries from the previous week that were later determined to be season-ending.

Matthews, who was sorely missed in the fourth quarter as the Redskins rallied from a 10-point deficit, sat out the following week and referred to the team collectively as "the walking wounded."

All the bad news would have been easier to swallow had Mason Crosby's 53-yard field goal in the final seconds of regulation not clanked off the upright. A successful kick also would have prevented Rodgers' overtime interception, the play that set up Washington for the game-winning points and led to the concussion, from ever happening.

If there was good news to be found, it's that it was still mid-October. The season wasn't yet half over, and there was time to regroup. McCarthy set the tone.

"We're going to get back, we're going to get our team healthy, we're going to get the guys ready to play next week," he said. "You can't control the injuries and we're not going to spend a whole lot of time discussing those types of things or worrying about them."

"I don't think it's becoming too much. It's a lot of guys going down, key guys, but from what I saw today, we've got guys that fight. That's what we need out of our guys."

– CB Tramon Williams

	1	2	3	4	OT
DOLPHINS	7	3	3	7	3
PACKERS	10	0	0	10	0

23

20

It was the third game out of four where a field goal sailing through the uprights in the final moments led to the Packers' downfall, this time at Lambeau Field against the Dolphins. The loss was a painful reprise of the week before at Washington, with the defeat coming again in overtime, and in both losses the Packers had an ineffective possession in the extra period.

It left Green Bay's players feeling the same frustration and muttering a familiar refrain when explaining the previous two losses—coming up short when victory was within reach. At the same time, QB Aaron Rodgers endured five sacks, Miami had a nearly 10-minute advantage in time of possession and over the last two games the Packers had converted only 5-of-26 on third downs.

Similar to the week before, even while keeping it close the Packers had earned the outcome, and most of the struggles had come on offense. A patchwork defense was holding its own despite weathering several injuries, with the inexperienced trio of linebacker Frank Zombo and defensive linemen C.J. Wilson and Jarius Wynn all putting in quality work vs. Miami.

Greg Jennings jetted through the Dolphins' secondary for a career-long 86-yard TD in the first quarter and finished with 133 yards on six catches. For the fifth-year veteran, the Miami game was a launching pad for his best NFL season statistically. After expressing his displeasure with the offense, he issued a warning.

"Time is of the essence," Jennings said. "Every win is important. At the end of the year, these are the type of games—this one, last week, Chicago—you look back and say, 'Man, if we could have got that one, where would we have possibly, potentially been?'"

Little did he know.

> We have to figure something out offensively and help our defense out a little bit. I think they've played well enough to win the last two weeks and we just haven't gotten the job done. When the defense is holding the other team to 16 last week and 23 this week, we feel like we should win those games.
>
> – QB Aaron Rodgers

GAME 7

	1	2	3	4	
VIKINGS	7	10	7	0	24
PACKERS	7	7	14	0	28

The stage was set for another Brett Favre miracle at Lambeau Field, and for another gut-wrenching loss for the Packers in 2010. Green Bay couldn't afford either and stubbornly averted both.

Three interceptions of Favre, including one returned for a score by Desmond Bishop, staked the Packers to an 11-point lead, in position to turn their season around and finally defeat their iconic quarterback in enemy colors. A flawless Favre didn't throw a single interception in beating the Packers twice for the Vikings in 2009, and he nearly overcame his miscues in this one.

A TD catch by Randy Moss late in the third quarter pulled Minnesota within four points, and Favre drove the Vikings all the way to the Green Bay 20-yard line in the final two minutes. But after an apparent touchdown pass to Percy Harvin in the back of the end zone was overturned by replay, Favre overthrew Moss in the end zone on fourth down.

Immediately after breathing a collective sigh of relief, the 71,000-plus broke into a boisterous celebration as they exited that echoed throughout the bowels of Lambeau. Favre had not gotten the upper hand this time, and a season on the verge of derailing after consecutive overtime losses was suddenly back on track.

"We all have the intestinal fortitude to pull these games out," nose tackle B.J. Raji said. "Early in the season it didn't go our way. Tonight it did. This was a long time coming. I'm glad we got this one. Hopefully we can continue this like we did last year and get on a roll."

The 28-24 victory began a four-game winning streak that thrust the Packers back into playoff contention.

"An excellent team win and an excellent character win," Head Coach Mike McCarthy said. "It was definitely something that we needed."

"These guys show so much heart, so much dedication just to go out there and fight, fight, fight 'til the end. This team can battle through anything.

– S Nick Collins

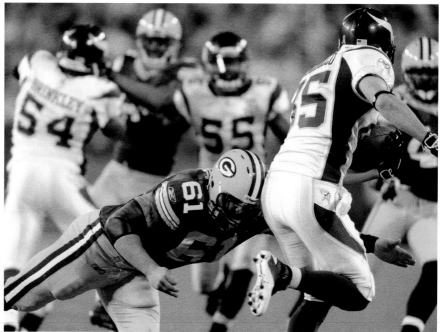

	1	2	3	4	
PACKERS	3	0	0	6	**9**
N.Y. JETS	0	0	0	0	**0**

 s two of the NFL's top defenses traded jabs, it was an unexpected source—Green Bay punter Tim Masthay—that packed the biggest punch. In the eighth NFL contest of his career, Masthay had what Head Coach Mike McCarthy called one of the finest kicking performances he had ever witnessed.

On a blustery day when he repeatedly punted out of his own territory, Masthay averaged 44 yards on eight punts, with a net of 41.5. Field position ruled in the defensive stalemate and he pinned five punts inside the 20, the most for a Green Bay punter since 1978. By tilting the field repeatedly, the Jets ended the game with zero return yards, and Masthay was presented with a game ball by the coaching staff.

Masthay was named the NFC Special Teams Player of the Week three days later, the first Packers' punter to win the award since 1994.

It was a banner outing and a turning point for a player who had worked to find his footing previously, but emerged as a weapon for the rest of 2010. Masthay dropped 20 punts inside the 20 over the final nine games of the regular season after doing so only five times before traveling to New York.

With less than four minutes remaining against the Jets and the Packers clinging to a 6-0 lead, Masthay banged a towering 41-yard punt that trickled out of bounds at the New York 23. The Jets failed to convert on fourth-and-11 and Mason Crosby's 40-yard field goal four plays later made the outcome no longer in doubt.

It was the first shutout for the Packers on the road since Oct. 27, 1991, and it was the first road win over the Jets in franchise history. The win also put Green Bay atop the NFC North at 5-3.

> It's a big win for us, one of the biggest I have been a part of in my time here, to go on the road and beat a team like this. Obviously offensively we would have liked to have done a little bit better, but our defense played incredible. Tim Masthay did an incredible job punting, Mason Crosby made three big kicks, and that's a big win for us.

– QB Aaron Rodgers

GAME 9

	1	2	3	4	
COWBOYS	0	7	0	0	**7**
PACKERS	0	28	7	10	**45**

The offense had shown flashes of potential in the first eight games and the Packers defense had matured into a withering blend of blitzes, stunts and turnovers for opponents. At kickoff of Week 9 vs. Dallas, however, Green Bay had yet to show what it was capable of when the offense, defense and special teams were firing in unison.

The Cowboys, wounded and struggling at 1-6, were the first witnesses of 2010, and it came in the second quarter. The Packers reeled off 28 points—the club's highest output in a quarter since 1992—with three long drives capped by short scoring tosses by QB Aaron Rodgers and another TD when Nick Collins raced 26 yards after a fumble on a kickoff return.

The second half provided more fireworks, starting with a 49-yard kick return by Sam Shields. On a third-quarter touchdown march Rodgers would connect on five passes for 61 yards to give Green Bay a 35-7 lead. After a field goal early in the fourth quarter, the lead would grow to 38 points when Clay Matthews sprinted 62 yards for a touchdown after an interception. In all, the offense posted four touchdowns and the defense and special teams added one TD each.

This was finally the Packers at their best. Even after gutting out a victory against Minnesota in their previous appearance at Lambeau Field and shutting out the Jets the week before, players were left wondering previously when it would all come together. That wasn't the case any longer. It was the kind of performance they had been working for.

"You always strive to play a complete game," Head Coach Mike McCarthy said. "We accomplished that tonight. The defense just swarmed all over them, kept them out of the end zone, and the offense got into a rhythm. We played a complete football game."

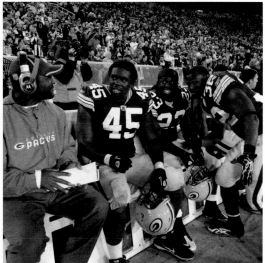

> "None of us are surprised. We knew we could do this. We knew we could get it going in the right direction. We're definitely not where we want to be, and we still have some steps to take to get there. It's understandable with how things were going early in the year, how many guys got banged up, that we'd have some doubters."
>
> – LB A.J. Hawk

 31

	1	2	3	4
PACKERS	0	17	7	7
VIKINGS	3	0	0	0

3

GAME 10

SUNDAY, NOVEMBER 21, 2010
HHH Metrodome • Attendance 64,120

" Greg is one of the best receivers in the league. We are very fortunate and blessed to have him on our team. When you throw just a comeback to him and he turns it into a big-time touchdown, it makes you look like a lot better quarterback. "

– QB Aaron Rodgers

It was just a little flick of Aaron Rodgers' wrist, his left wrist in fact, but it showed how in sync he and receiver Greg Jennings were at the Metrodome.

In the second quarter with the score tied at 3, the Packers were on the Vikings' 11-yard line threatening to score the game's first touchdown. Rodgers went back to pass, spun away from defensive end Jared Allen, and rolled to his left.

Keeping his eyes downfield, Rodgers ever-so-subtly motioned with his left hand for Jennings, who was mirroring Rodgers, to step back the other way. With no hesitation, Rodgers fired and Jennings was sitting in the perfect opening in the end zone to haul it in.

Minnesota cornerback Antoine Winfield could only tear off his chinstrap in disgust and frustration. Rodgers and Jennings were on the same page, and there was no stopping them.

Jennings went on to catch two more TD passes, including a short hitch he turned into a 46-yard score, for the first three-touchdown game of his career. Rodgers would throw four TDs in all for a regular-season career first of his own, and his passer rating of 141.3 was a season best.

"When he gets in a zone like that, there is no quarterback better," Jennings said. "He is so accurate, able to extend plays with his legs, then he can run when you give him the lane. He puts a lot of pressure on the defense."

So does Jennings, whose season-high 152 receiving yards continued a dominant stretch in which he averaged six catches for 109 yards over a seven-game span. He caught eight of his 12 regular-season TDs during that time.

The Packers' 31-3 romp over the Vikings concluded a season sweep of the border rivals for the first time since 2007 and gave Green Bay four straight wins.

 **17**

		1	2	3	4		**20**
	PACKERS	3	0	7	7		
	FALCONS	3	7	0	10		

D own by 7 points with 5:59 on the clock and 90 yards of Georgia Dome turf in front of them, the Packers stepped into the offensive huddle with this NFC heavyweight showdown on the line.

Sixteen plays later they found the end zone to tie the score. Although a long kickoff return and a facemask penalty would set up the Falcons for a last-second field goal, the offense had proven it could execute on the road in the most trying of circumstances, foreshadowing the playoff run that was to begin in six weeks.

Neglected by history due to the game's outcome, the epic drive was among the most impressive of the season. Quarterback Aaron Rodgers, who regrettably fumbled on a goal-line sneak earlier, completed eight passes to five different receivers. Rookie tight end Andrew Quarless caught two for 30 yards. Running back Brandon Jackson's three receptions and two rushes accounted for 23 yards.

The offense didn't even encounter a third down until it had almost reached the red zone. It also had to overcome two false starts and a sack, meaning the drive actually required more than 100 total yards.

Most dramatically, Rodgers converted two fourth downs. The first was from the Atlanta 21, when he improvised a shovel pass to James Jones to make it first-and-goal. The second was do-or-die from the 10 with 1:06 left, and Rodgers scrambled to his left to buy time as Jordy Nelson broke open cutting across the end zone to Rodgers' left.

Deftly, Rodgers looked back the other way so as not to telegraph the bullet he was about to fire, and when he pulled the trigger, the velocity alone made hair stand on end. Nelson made a tremendous catch just inside the boundary, got both feet down, and a gigantic building block for the postseason run had been laid.

> I thought Aaron Rodgers played huge today. He had the one play he wishes he could have back, but just the way he played with his feet, extended plays, handled their pressure, the no-huddle and the operation of the huddle, he did an outstanding job. You want to walk away with victories, No. 1, but that was probably one of his better individual performances.
>
> – Head Coach Mike McCarthy

	1	2	3	4
49ERS	3	10	3	0
PACKERS	0	14	14	6

SF 16   34

GAME 12

SUNDAY, DECEMBER 5, 2010
Lambeau Field • Attendance 70,575

The veteran wide receiver had been quiet for too long on the field, and in recent weeks he had seen his streaks snapped for both consecutive games played and games with a reception. Donald Driver had been hobbled by a battered right leg that was listed with two separate injuries. His familiar cackle wasn't filling the locker room.

There were whispers that maybe the big plays that had become Driver's trademark over the last decade were no longer part of his repertoire after 12 seasons. He hadn't found the end zone in six contests.

Driver put that conversation to rest in his blue-and-gold throwback uniform against the 49ers on the fourth play of the second half. He scored a rambling 61-yard TD by hauling in a strike at the San Francisco 40, immediately breaking a tackle, ducking another defender 5 yards later, running through a third tackler at the 10 and churning through four 49ers at the goal line.

It was one of the Packers' most spectacular plays of 2010, and QB Aaron Rodgers called it "one of the best plays I've ever been a part of." It increased Green Bay's lead to 21-13 and energized the team, which would score on its next three possessions to pull away from San Francisco.

It showed there was plenty of spark left in those slender legs. After his 14th career grab of over 50 yards, a smiling Driver took a parting shot at the crowd of media gathered around him following the game.

"You guys think I am 35 and I am done," he said. "Today was an opportunity, and when I got the ball, I wanted to make the best of it. I think at the end of the day, all you guys shook your head and said, 'Well, I guess he has still got it.'"

> "Donald Driver's touchdown was the biggest play in the game. I thought it ignited our team. We needed that. We had some segments there in the first half where we weren't as sharp as we needed to be. But Donald's play was clearly the biggest and then we were able to take off from there.

– Head Coach Mike McCarthy

63

GAME 13

	1	2	3	4	
PACKERS	0	0	3	0	3
LIONS	0	0	0	7	7

The concern coming from the Packers' locker room was from more than just being unable to generate more than three points, squandering a prime opportunity to step forward in the playoff race or having a 10-game winning streak against Detroit snapped. Those issues deepened when late in the first half quarterback Aaron Rodgers was knocked from the game with a concussion, his second of 2010.

The hit that briefly changed Rodgers' season came with just over three minutes remaining in the second quarter. Rodgers scrambled for 18 yards—the Packers' longest rush of the game—did not slide and was dropped to the turf by a pair of solid hits. He was slow to rise, stayed in the game and was sacked on the next play. After completing a 4-yard pass on third-and-17, Rodgers did not return.

Rodgers suffered his first concussion in Week 5 against Washington, came back the next week and had been in top form since with 14 TD passes and only three interceptions. But this second concussion would keep him from the following game at New England and became part of the club's storyline for the rest of the year.

Matt Flynn replaced Rodgers at Detroit, but Green Bay was only able to score a field goal in the third quarter. It was the club's lowest scoring output since 2006. The Packers, who had three turnovers, were also only able to post 258 yards of total offense, their lowest total since Week 1 of 2009. The team's three running backs combined for 31 yards on 15 carries. The Lions had shown in 2010 that they were emerging from the NFC North cellar.

Head Coach Mike McCarthy would make a daring call on the Packers' final offensive play, a deep pass to Greg Jennings on fourth-and-1 from the Detroit 31, but the toss from Flynn fell out of the wide receiver's reach with just under a minute remaining.

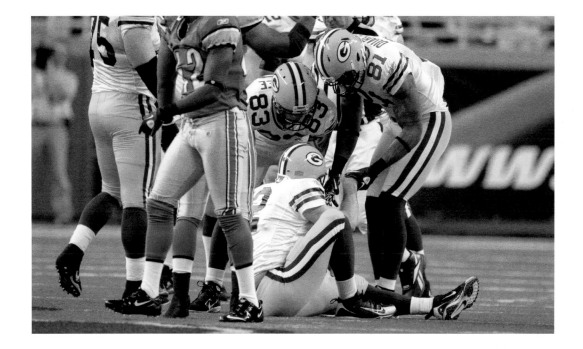

> " With the people we have on this offense, it doesn't matter if it's the second-string quarterback or the seventh-string quarterback. With the people we have, you don't put up three points. That's ridiculous. "
>
> – WR James Jones

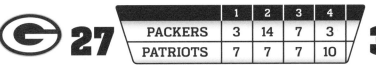

	1	2	3	4
PACKERS	3	14	7	3
PATRIOTS	7	7	7	10

27      31

Heeding the words of Head Coach Mike McCarthy, the Packers were nobody's underdog in Foxboro, Mass.

Subbing for a concussed Aaron Rodgers, backup quarterback Matt Flynn made his first NFL start and validated the team's belief in him with 251 yards passing and three touchdowns, far more productive numbers than counterpart and three-time Super Bowl champion Tom Brady.

"We knew what he was capable of," receiver Greg Jennings said. "We were hoping as an offense we didn't hold back just because Matt was in, and we didn't."

The Packers grabbed the lead three different times, held the ball for more than 40 minutes, and made the Patriots look nothing like the invincible outfit that had lambasted the Jets and Bears by a combined 81-10 the previous two weeks.

Still, it wasn't enough as Green Bay's final drive came up 15 yards short and Flynn was sacked on fourth down, handing the Patriots a 31-27 decision and the Packers their sixth loss by four points or less.

"I thought our team fought extremely hard," McCarthy said. "They are definitely warriors. I'm proud of them for that."

Curiously, though, the mood in the locker room began turning from somber to optimistic before many had even processed this second straight road defeat.

As reporters entered for interviews, they were the first to inform some of the players that earlier results that day—namely the Eagles' comeback from a 21-point deficit with eight minutes left against the Giants, and the Lions' overtime triumph against the Buccaneers—had put the Packers, despite an 8-6 record, in control of their playoff fate with two home games remaining.

The sixth and final seed in the NFC was all that was available, and it would take two wins to grab it. The next two weeks were suddenly all that mattered.

> "We didn't believe the hype coming into the game that we didn't have a chance. We knew we could beat them and we just fell short. If we play the rest of the season like that, things will fall our way. Just play with the energy and intensity we played with today.
>
> – DE Ryan Pickett

17

		1	2	3	4
N.Y. GIANTS		0	14	3	0
PACKERS		14	7	10	14

45

As the showdown with the Giants loomed, Head Coach Mike McCarthy stressed to the team that despite being 8-6 and coming off consecutive losses, all of their goals were still in front of them. There was no doubting the urgency. For Green Bay the playoffs had arrived. At 9-5, New York was in similar circumstances.

Returning was quarterback Aaron Rodgers, who hadn't played in six quarters because of a concussion. Fitted with a new helmet and looking extremely sharp in practice, Rodgers zipped the ball around with such velocity that his teammates credited it to a rested arm. The Giants were countering with a defense that was among the NFL's best at rushing the quarterback.

It wouldn't matter. On the first play of the Packers' second possession, Rodgers shook off the rust by throwing an 80-yard TD to Jordy Nelson. The quarterback was off to what he deemed at the time the best performance of his career, strafing the Giants repeatedly downfield while completing 25-of-37 for 404 yards and four touchdowns, for a passer rating of 139.9.

"Man, he's special," said wide receiver Greg Jennings, who had seven grabs for 142 yards. "He's back. He's definitely back."

Rodgers wasn't alone as the Packers overwhelmed New York with season highs of 515 total yards and six defensive takeaways. Running back John Kuhn had a career-high three TDs. The defense intercepted Giants' QB Eli Manning four times, and though New York entered the game leading the NFL in time of possession, the Giants held the ball for only 22:59.

"We all knew the magnitude of a loss, and we knew we needed to win, and we knew we needed to look good doing it from a confidence standpoint," said nose tackle B.J. Raji. "I knew the type of guys we have. We don't back down. We don't fold."

“ We finally put together four quarters. I don't want to sound cocky, but if we can put together four quarters, we can do that to pretty much everybody. That's just the kind of talent and will we have on this team. Put four together like that, we're dangerous. ”

– LB Desmond Bishop

		1	2	3	4		
3	BEARS	0	3	0	0	**10**	
	PACKERS	0	0	3	7		

> The intensity that we played with today, we've got to keep playing with that intensity throughout the playoffs. We can't have a repeat of what happened last year. This playoff game, we've got to come out and play with the same fire we played with today, and good things will happen.

– CB Charles Woodson

The entire team crowded around him following practice five days before the Wild Card playoff at Philadelphia, after Mike McCarthy beckoned linebacker Erik Walden to the middle of the huddle. Then the head coach delivered the news: Walden had been named NFC Defensive Player of the Week for his performance in the finale vs. Chicago, and a hearty cheer erupted among his teammates.

It had been an improbable journey to the center of attention for Walden. His career had a lengthy transactions list when he was signed off the street by Green Bay Oct. 27—drafted 167th overall by Dallas in 2008, cut in training camp, claimed by the Chiefs and played in nine games that season, released, appeared in 19 games over three years for the Dolphins and waived again. Walden was signed by the Packers because of the team's long list of injuries at outside linebacker.

He quickly became a contributor on special teams, then made the first start of his career at New England and led the club with nine tackles. A few weeks later Walden was a terror against Chicago in the playoff-clinching victory with a team-high 16 stops, three sacks and five hits on QB Jay Cutler. Walden became the most unlikely of the seven linebackers in team history to earn the Player of the Week award.

Green Bay allowed Chicago just 117 net passing yards, with no touchdowns and two interceptions. The Bears, who had already sewn up the NFC North and a first-round bye, went hard to keep their traditional rivals out of the postseason by leaving their starters in for the entire contest. Nick Collins' late interception preserved a narrow victory and punched the Packers' ticket to the playoffs.

Walden's three sacks were part of six on the afternoon, giving Green Bay 47 on the season, the team's most since 2001. It also provided the third-year veteran from Middle Tennessee State, a player who like many of the Packers' acquisitions had traveled the hard road to NFL success, his first standing ovation.

G 21

	1	2	3	4	
PACKERS	7	7	7	0	
EAGLES	0	3	7	6	

16

Quarterback Aaron Rodgers and his fleet platoon of targets had been the foundation of the Packers' offensive fortunes in 2010, and the defense had proven itself to be among the NFL's elite by surrendering over 20 points in a contest only four times. In the NFC Wild Card playoff, those two constants were joined by rookie running back James Starks.

Starks showed a glimmer of his skills in December against San Francisco in his NFL debut, slashing for 73 yards. With the coaching staff demanding better fundamentals from the youthful runner, he had only carried the ball 11 times since. At Philadelphia a little over a month after his debut—where in the opener perennial rushing leader Ryan Grant was lost for the season to an ankle injury—Starks suddenly looked all grown up.

He set a franchise rookie postseason record with 123 yards on 23 attempts in a performance Rodgers called perhaps the most important factor in the win. Starks jumped out to a strong start, ripping off a 27-yard gain on his first carry, the key play on a 68-yard TD drive. On a windy afternoon in below-freezing temperatures, Starks provided punch to an offense that had lacked a formidable running game for most of 2010.

On all three Packers' scoring marches, Starks carried the ball at least four times. When Green Bay took a 7-0 lead, the running back had four rushes for 36 yards and a pair of receptions for 9 yards. When the Packers pushed ahead 21-10, Starks kept the possession moving with five attempts for 32 yards. If the playoffs demand a featured back that can carry the load, the Packers had finally found a leading man.

"He established a hot hand early and I rode it," said Head Coach Mike McCarthy. "James was a difference-maker."

It wasn't as if the trusty pillars of Green Bay's success—Rodgers and the league's fifth-ranked defense—didn't also prove to be significant in the outcome. The quarterback was sharp in his first postseason victory, recording a passer rating of 122.5 while completing 18-of-27 for 180 yards. Rodgers capped each touchdown drive with a scoring toss, and after fumbling to open the second half, his third-quarter TD march with a pair of key third-down strikes to Donald Driver quieted a rowdy Philly crowd.

The responsibility for closing out the win fell on the defense, fitting in a year when the unit repeatedly preserved victories. Philadelphia rallied from a 21-10 deficit in the fourth

quarter with a 75-yard drive, with quarterback Michael Vick's sneak on fourth-and-goal from the 1 making it 21-16 with 4:02 left. The Eagles failed to get the ensuing 2-point conversion, which proved to be a huge turn of events.

The Packers could only drain half of the remaining clock and punted back to the Eagles just after the 2-minute warning. Vick quickly drove Philadelphia to the Green Bay 27,

> "We've had a few ups and downs on this rollercoaster of a year, but hopefully we're peaking at the right time. Three wins in a row, all playoff-like environments in which we need to win or else we go home. We feel good about where we're at. You can say we're dangerous, but we're just playing at the level we know how.
>
> – LB Clay Matthews

and with the clock ticking below 45 seconds, lofted a high pass to 6-foot-3 wide receiver Riley Cooper deep in the left side of the end zone. It was intercepted with both hands by leaping cornerback Tramon Williams, who was in perfect position.

"We feel like our defense, if we are in a pressure situation, can go out there and perform and get off the field," said cornerback Charles Woodson. "Today we came up with the big stop at the end."

		1	2	3	4	
	PACKERS	0	28	14	6	48
	FALCONS	7	7	0	7	21

In the week leading up to the NFC Divisional playoff game in Atlanta, quarterback Aaron Rodgers admitted he likes playing in domes because he gets to wear his favorite shoes.

Those comfortable feet, as well as Rodgers' right arm of course, put on quite a show as the Packers not only defeated but dominated the NFC's No. 1 seed.

Repeatedly, Rodgers dodged pass-rushers to both avoid sacks and deliver pinpoint throws that led the Packers to touchdowns on five consecutive offensive possessions. Time after time, the Georgia Dome crowd rose in anticipation of a big hit as a blind-side rusher closed in on Rodgers, only to sit back down in exasperation as he somehow spun free and found one of four receivers who contributed between 75 and 101 yards on the night.

Rodgers' final numbers were too good for a postseason contest: 31-of-36, 366 yards, three TDs passing, one TD rushing, and a 136.8 rating. Quarterbacks aren't supposed to be capable of that in the playoffs, especially on the road.

Within the locker room, there was no surprise at what he had done. Outside the team, the performance made believers out of those who wondered whether Rodgers could dance on the biggest of stages. He could, and it wasn't just the shoes.

"We're dangerous, and we knew that," receiver Donald Driver said. "It's a scary thing. When we're clicking, we're unstoppable."

The Packers went from trailing 7-0 with five minutes remaining in the first quarter to leading 42-14 with under three minutes left in the third, or in just a little more than half a game.

Accompanying Rodgers' mastery during that time were two momentum-turning plays by Tramon Williams, the defensive star for the second straight week.

Coming off his Wild Card-clinching interception in Philadelphia, Williams picked off two more passes on back-to-back Falcons drives late in the second quarter that eliminated any Atlanta hopes of winning a shootout.

First, Williams displayed his underrated athletic ability by outjumping Michael Jenkins on a deep ball to the end zone to prevent the Falcons from breaking a 14-all tie. Then, with Atlanta trying to sneak closer to field-goal range on the final play of the first half, he employed his painstaking film study.

Recognizing Atlanta's formation and quarterback Matt Ryan's short rollout to the left, Williams baited Ryan into trying to squeeze in a tight sideline throw to Roddy White. Ryan bit, Williams broke, and 70 yards later the up-and-coming corner was a postseason hero once again.

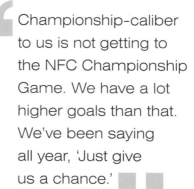

> **Championship-caliber to us is not getting to the NFC Championship Game. We have a lot higher goals than that. We've been saying all year, 'Just give us a chance.'**
> – LB A.J. Hawk

"That's the swing there," guard Daryn Colledge said of a 10-point shift on the fateful snap, one Atlanta head coach Mike Smith didn't want to risk, having initially called for the field goal before deciding to run another play. "That's the one that puts you over the top."

Or, in the bigger picture, gets you halfway there.

"We've had 16 quarters on our mind, and we've completed eight of them," Head Coach Mike McCarthy said. "We feel very good about who we are, the way we've played, our brand of football in all three areas. And that's what we're sticking to."

G 21

	1	2	3	4
PACKERS	7	7	0	7
BEARS	0	0	0	14

14

One nearly turned into a touchdown, another became one, and two prevented possible scores.

Four interceptions and their ramifications decided the NFC Championship, just the second playoff meeting ever between storied rivals Green Bay and Chicago. The role each played in the Packers' 21-14 victory should never be undersold.

The one near-touchdown kept the Bears in the game, but thanks to some hustle and grit didn't turn things Chicago's way. In command up 14-0 early in the third quarter, the Packers faced third-and-goal from the Chicago 6-yard line, seemingly sure to boost their advantage.

But Aaron Rodgers forced a throw over the middle that Chicago linebacker Brian Urlacher picked off. Urlacher raced downfield, with Rodgers possessing the only viable pursuit angle.

His form less than instruction-worthy, Rodgers caught up and dove in front of Urlacher's legs. Reaching back as Urlacher swerved to jump over him, Rodgers barely tripped him up to terminate a possible 94-yard return at 39 yards.

"I don't get paid to tackle," Rodgers said, "but that was probably one of my better plays of the day."

The best play of nose tackle B.J. Raji's career came one quarter later. Unable to capitalize on Urlacher's turnover, the Bears eventually climbed within 14-7 but faced third-and-5 from their 15 with just over six minutes to play.

Defensive coordinator Dom Capers hadn't called "Right Cat" all season, but his unit executed the zone blitz perfectly. Right cornerback Sam Shields, already with a sack and forced fumble in the game, charged Caleb Hanie's blind side, and the third-string QB—in for an injured starter and ineffective backup—never anticipated a 340-pound lineman feigning a rush and defending running back Matt Forté's short crossing route. Raji intercepted the ball and waltzed 18 yards to the end zone, re-establishing Green Bay's two-score lead.

"He steps into the line to use a lineman's block, and then he pops out late into the throwing lane," Capers said of Raji's duties on the play. "Many times the quarterback won't see a lineman popping out."

Perhaps the last thing the Bears expected to see was a rookie cornerback sending their archrivals to the Super Bowl.

An undrafted speedster who played corner only one season in college, Shields from the start had "no fear," according to veteran Charles Woodson, and emerged as the defense's vital nickelback by the end of training camp. He came of age in Week 9 with an acrobatic, one-handed grab for the first of two regular-season interceptions, and he doubled that total in the biggest game of his life.

"We just always believed in ourselves if we had the opportunity to get in the playoffs, that it didn't matter what road, which way we had to go, we felt confident we could get it done. Three tough games, three tough places.

– CB Charles Woodson

First, Shields ran stride-for-stride with Johnny Knox in the final minute of the first half and leaped to intercept a deep ball near the goal line, preserving the Packers' 14-point halftime lead. Then, in the waning moments of the game on fourth-and-5 from the Green Bay 29 and the Bears down only 7, Shields undercut Knox on a seam route and snagged his second interception, sealing the NFC title.

"To win big games like this, it comes down—and I've said this many times before—to two or three or four plays a game," Capers said. "We were fortunate to make those plays."

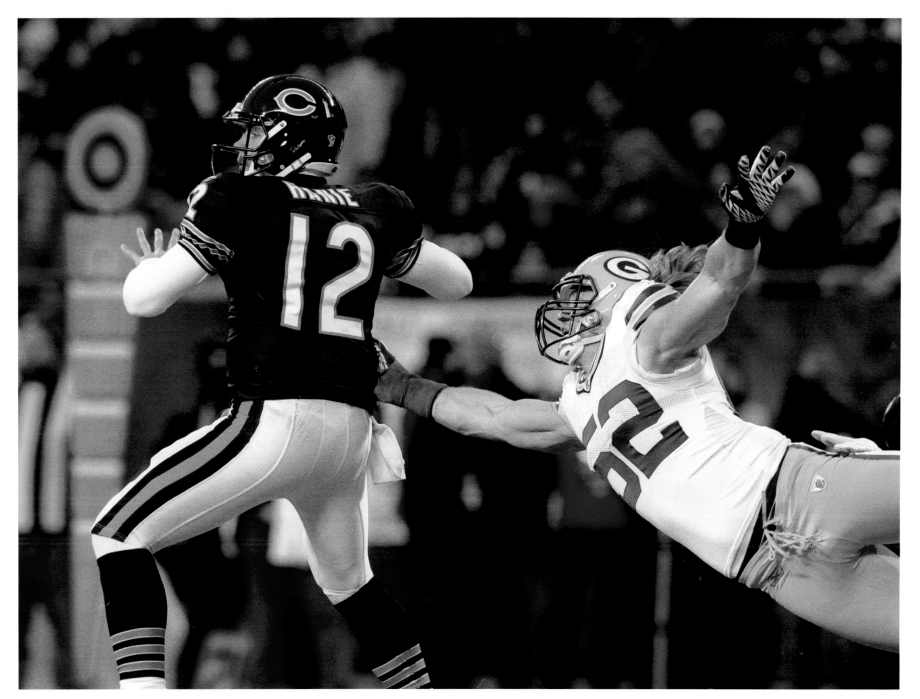

SUPER BOWL XLV

SUNDAY, FEBRUARY 6, 2011
Cowboys Stadium • Attendance 91,060

The Packers had the turnover margin decidedly in their favor, the quarterback to make the clutch throws, and the inspiration to see it through.

A foolproof recipe, perhaps, or simply the right ingredients for this team at this time. Either way, the result was the fourth Super Bowl title and 13th NFL championship in franchise history, a 31-25 triumph over the Pittsburgh Steelers in Super Bowl XLV at Cowboys Stadium in North Texas.

Statistically, the difference was undeniably the turnovers. Green Bay's defense created three while the offense committed none. Moreover, those three Pittsburgh miscues were converted into 21 points, forcing the Steelers to play uphill throughout.

Defensive coordinator Dom Capers preaches that turnovers require a collective effort, and the Super Bowl reinforced that.

In the first quarter, defensive end Howard Green got pressure on Pittsburgh quarterback Ben Roethlisberger—and a piece of his arm—as he tried to throw deep to Mike Wallace, and the ensuing floater was picked off by safety Nick Collins and returned 37 yards for a score.

In the second quarter, rookie cornerback Sam Shields had outside leverage on Wallace, forcing him to cut over the middle. Reserve Jarrett Bush was waiting there to cut him off and make a diving stab of an ill-advised throw for the defense's eighth interception of the postseason.

Most critically, on the first play of the fourth quarter, linebacker Clay Matthews sensed a run was coming his way and told defensive end Ryan Pickett to "spill it" to the outside. Pickett obliged, allowing Matthews to pop the ball loose from running back Rashard Mendenhall, with linebacker Desmond Bishop recovering.

That last turnover was the game-changer. The Steelers had rallied from a 21-3 deficit to within 21-17 and had second-and-2 on the Green Bay 33-yard line when their comeback was abruptly halted.

"Nothing neutralizes that momentum more than a takeaway," Capers said.

Nothing keeps it more than a perfectly placed throw, and Aaron Rodgers had his share on his way to MVP honors. It may forever be argued which pass was his best, but having three prime candidates speaks to Rodgers' brilliance in this game.

He threaded one over the middle between safeties Ryan Clark and Troy Polamalu to receiver Greg Jennings for a 21-yard touchdown in the second quarter, with Jennings absorbing a big hit from Polamalu at the goal line.

He found receiver Jordy Nelson on an important third-and-10, moments after the Mendenhall fumble and one snap after Nelson, heavily targeted due to Donald Driver's ankle injury, had dropped the ball on a similar route. This one went for 38 yards to set up Jennings' second TD.

"He played OK," Jennings deadpanned. "Hey, he's at the helm for a reason."

The Packers still needed one more defensive stop, just as they did in two of their three playoff triumphs, but getting it without two banged-up defenders in Shields and veteran cornerback Charles Woodson didn't phase them.

The team had overcome injuries throughout the year, and the Super Bowl continued that story. Just as the offense stayed on course when Driver went down early, the defense owed it to Woodson not to fold.

> " I feel a sense of pride in the guys in this locker room. I've said this over and over—a team is something very, very special, and a championship team that goes through all the things this one went through is remarkably special. "
>
> – GM Ted Thompson

Playing in his 13th season still chasing an elusive title, Woodson had unified the team with his now-famous "One" speech in the locker room immediately following the NFC Championship. He continued to inspire at halftime of the Super Bowl with the few words he was able to get out, knowing his broken collarbone would prevent him from playing the second half.

"I think I let out all of my emotions at halftime," Woodson said. "They understood how much I wanted it."

His teammates came through, as fellow cornerback Tramon Williams capped a brilliant postseason by breaking up a fourth-and-5 pass to Wallace from the Pittsburgh 33 with 49 seconds left.

Another title was won for Titletown. The Vince Lombardi Trophy was coming home.

"The name on that trophy, that means a lot to us," nose tackle B.J. Raji said, "and we can't wait to bring it back to Green Bay."

Most impressively, Rodgers didn't hold back on an even more crucial third-and-10 from his own 25, leading by only three and six minutes remaining.

"We were by no means conservative," Head Coach Mike McCarthy said. "No regrets, no excuses."

As Jennings ran a deep post, Rodgers rifled a throw so hard that even though it grazed the fingertip of cornerback Ike Taylor, it stayed on course for Jennings to haul it in. The 31-yard gain set up a field goal for the game's final points.

AFTERWORD Mark Murphy

The 2010 season was truly special for the Packers, and I was so proud of how our team performed all year. The victory over the Steelers in Super Bowl XLV marked the team's 13th world championship—an NFL record—and fourth Super Bowl title. For the organization, it was an exceptional achievement, and for our fans, another source of tremendous pride.

Our team showed great character all season in overcoming tremendous adversity, particularly with 15 players ending the season on injured reserve. In all my years playing and working in the NFL I've never witnessed such an effort. It is a tribute to Ted Thompson and his staff, as well as Mike McCarthy and his coaching staff. Never once were injuries used as an excuse.

In a year of ups and downs, it was remarkable how well our team responded to hardship. Whenever we faced a challenge, we bounced back strong. After a couple of disappointing overtime losses, we had a big, emotional win against the Vikings, and then went on the road to beat a talented Jets team in a tough environment. Similarly, after a loss in Detroit, we played well at New England and took the league's best team to the wire behind our backup quarterback. To me, even though it was a loss, it served as a turning point and set the stage for our remarkable run. With our backs against the wall and needing to win our last two games of the season to make the playoffs, our team delivered.

The playoffs seemed to happen so fast; they almost had a surreal quality to them. As the sixth seed, we had to win three straight games on the road in order to get to the Super Bowl. Our players and coaches rose to the challenge. I always had the confidence that our team was going to win.

It was an extraordinary moment to be on the field as the clock wound down in the Super Bowl. The elation following the victory was infectious. Everyone, including the fans that made the trip, felt it. It was tremendous to see the joy of the players and coaches after having put in so much work and persevered through so many difficult moments.

My son, Brian, was able to join me. I'm not sure how he got down on the field, but he did. It was a special experience to share with him, both on the field and later in the locker room. It brought me full circle to a moment I had with my father; after I'd won Super Bowl XVII as a player with the Washington Redskins, my father somehow made his way into our locker room, where we shared a memorable celebration.

That victorious Packers locker room brought back a lot of memories. It's so difficult to win a Super Bowl, and the celebration behind closed doors has a different, more

120

intimate quality with the smaller group compared to being out with the masses on the field. The postgame party back at our hotel is kind of a blur—everyone was celebrating, Kid Rock performed, players danced—but I have a vivid memory of Coach McCarthy up on stage with the Lombardi Trophy.

Even on the flight back to Green Bay the next morning, everyone was still on a high and excited. We knew there would be people welcoming us back, but we weren't certain how many. The fans still came out, some even on snowmobiles. It was remarkable to see so many people, especially as we got closer to Lambeau Field. Standing with the trophy near the front of the first bus, Coach McCarthy and I kept looking at each other and saying, "Can you believe this?"

The next day's Return to Titletown event at Lambeau Field was incredibly special. I remember it being bitterly cold; I underdressed for the weather, but the excitement and passion in the air kept me warm. Even with the chilly temperature, our fans filled the stadium to share in the celebration.

The ring ceremony brought us all back together, and the mood in the room was giddy. What I said to everybody that night was that this team was now part of the rich legacy of the Green Bay Packers. There is not a team in league that has more tradition and history, and for that we could all be proud.

Prior to the NFC Championship Game, President Barack Obama—a Bears fan—said that if Chicago won the game, he would attend the Super Bowl. Those plans changed when we beat the Bears. In the locker room afterward Charles Woodson said that if the president didn't want to come "watch us win the Super Bowl then guess what: We'll go see him!"

Our trip to the White House was an unforgettable experience for everyone. To be able to represent the Packers organization, the city of Green Bay and the greatest fans in the NFL was remarkable. I know everyone involved will cherish that time with the president and the opportunity to visit such a historic landmark.

I have now experienced Super Bowl wins both as a player and also as a member of the front office. As a player, your focus is on the team and the coaches. As team president, I have a much better sense of how difficult it is to win a title and how much goes into building a championship team. Every member of the organization has a role. Much more is involved, and I now have a broader view and appreciation of this achievement. In some ways, this Super Bowl victory has been more satisfying.

It was a special season, no doubt about it. The players, coaches, organization and Packers fans everywhere can look back and take great pride in the accomplishment. Meantime, we are looking forward to capturing our next title and bringing another Lombardi Trophy home.

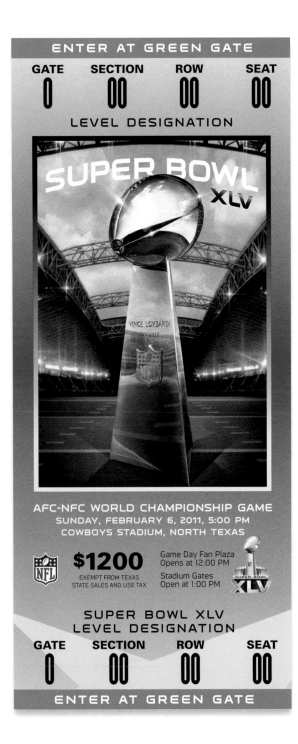

ACKNOWLEDGEMENTS

GREEN BAY PACKERS

PROJECT DIRECTOR
Tim Connolly

PROJECT MANAGER
Aaron Popkey

WRITERS
Mike Spofford, Ricky Zeller

PROJECT CONTRIBUTORS
Jonathan Butnick, Tom Fanning, Kate Hogan,
Kelsey Kroll, Joan Malcheski and Sarah Quick

SKYBOX PRESS

PUBLISHER
Peter Gotfredson

EDITOR
Scott Gummer

CREATIVE DIRECTOR
Nate Beale

COPYEDITOR
Victoria Scavo

SKYBOX PRESS wishes to thank Jerry Hanson and Pam Burnett, Debbie King and the NFL, Chris Poitras and Jostens, Ken Coburn and the team at Global Interprint, Donald Van Giesen, and our sincere thanks to Dean McCausland and Don McCall

Cataloging-in-Publication Data has been applied for and may be obtained from the Library of Congress.

ISBN 978-1-4197-0295-2

Printed proudly in Wisconsin
10 9 8 7 6 5 4 3 2 1

Published by Skybox Press, an imprint of Luxury Custom Publishing
Distributed in North America by Abrams, an imprint of ABRAMS

3920 Conde Street
San Diego, CA 92110
www.skyboxpress.com

115 West 18th Street
New York, NY 10011
www.abramsbooks.com